Social Anxiety

How to Overcome Shyness, Be More Confident and Live Your Life to the Fullest

Sara Elliott Price

Published in The USA by:

Success Life Publishing

125 Thomas Burke Dr.

Hillsborough, NC 27278

ISBN-10: 1511851112

Disclaimer

Table of Contents

Introduction

Do you envy people who go about their lives able to just be themselves? They don't seem to care what they look like, what they sound like or what others think of them. Bold and assertive or calm and serene, they appear to have everything under control.

Well, this may come as a surprise to you, but things are not always what they seem. No one really knows what goes on in the minds of other people. An estimated four out of every ten of us, mainly but not only women, have problems with self-confidence, ranging from slight nervousness to acute shyness to social phobia, including agoraphobia. It's just that many of these people have learned how to manage their fears.

However, for every person who succeeds in overcoming their nerves to speak in public or who has battled through issues of low self-esteem, there's another who isn't managing too well. Some of these people get by, provided they don't actually have to hold a conversation with anyone; others struggle with alcohol, drug abuse or depression, and may be too anxious even to leave the house.

If you have social anxiety you are afraid of being the center of attention and having people look at you. You hate the idea of being watched, analyzed or criticized, and have a fear of embarrassing yourself in front of others. You worry about meeting new people and find it hard to go into stores and restaurants or even walk down the street. You can't hold a conversation, and find it impossible to assert yourself.

This book looks at social anxiety and what can be done to resolve it. We'll take a look at why we get anxious and what stops us making progress, before examining practical solutions that can help someone with social anxiety learn to overcome their fears.

Chapter 1: The Origins of Anxiety

We're going to start by taking a quick look at the general subject of anxiety. Then we'll be turning our attention more specifically to social anxiety, where it comes from and how it develops, because experts believe that knowing the source of our anxiety is an important part of learning to overcome it.

Why do we worry? Is it normal? Are humans just programmed to get anxious?

Well, a certain amount of anxiety is normal. It's linked to fear, usually based on previous experience. If you were mugged after work one dark evening, you'd understandably be anxious about it happening again. So anxiety can be a normal response to a dangerous situation. It can help you avoid the situation you're worried about and prompt you to make arrangements to stop it happening again, like leaving work earlier or making sure you're with someone else.

On the other hand, a lot of the things we're anxious about have never actually happened to us and in fact will probably never happen, like being swept up in a tornado or being struck by lightning. We're influenced by what we see on the TV or read in the newspapers. And let's face it, many of the things we worry about are so trivial they wouldn't matter much even if they did happen, like blurting out something inappropriate in front of others or not knowing what to say to people. It's embarrassing, but it's not like it's the end of the world.

But sometimes it feels almost as bad. The fear of humiliating ourselves through something relatively trivial, like making a social blunder, can be crippling. This type of anxiety is both pointless and damaging, leading to depression and isolation, eating disorders, alcohol or drug abuse and even agoraphobia. Doctors refer to this type of extreme anxiety as an "anxiety disorder," and if directed specifically at social situations (as against worrying about something happening, like being struck by lightning) it's called "social anxiety disorder," or "social phobia."

The anxiety factors

So how come some people are happy go lucky, and others suffer from anxiety? Experts believe that a combination of at least two of three different factors can influence whether you become a "worrier": your genes, your parents and your experiences. Let's take a brief look at each one.

Your genes: The tendency to worry can run in families. You might have picked up on anxiety in others as you grew up, or simply have inherited a tendency to react to situations by developing anxiety. This is especially true about social anxiety.

Jon's parents were not great mixers, and his mother especially was self-conscious and nervous in public. No surprise then that Jon was also shy and tongue-tied when he had to talk to anyone. After surviving years of taunting and isolation at school, it was only when Jon left home and started living independently that he began to make friends, gain in confidence and break free of this anxiety.

Your parents: Mistaken parenting styles can make children grow into anxious adults. Over-protective parents who don't allow their kids to be exposed to any threat or danger, real or imaginary, are not helping them learn to cope in the real world. Controlling parents who make every decision for their children leave them with dependency issues, ill-equipped for an independent life. And inconsistent parents make for insecure children who are uncertain and anxious as adults.

Your experiences: Some of us go through a very traumatic experience, either in childhood or as adults. Appalling events like child abuse, natural or man-made disasters, military service in a war zone, acts of terrorism, violent crime, and horrendous road traffic accidents – any of these things can be traumatic and can continue to affect us for years to come.

Norah was seriously abused as a child for many years, which left her psychologically traumatized. She had very low self-esteem and experienced difficulties in social situations even decades later. One result of her childhood experiences was that she avoided contact with others because she was afraid of friendly questions about her background and where she'd grown up. Unable to talk about it, this secret became a barrier against developing any kind of social relationships.

Look again at those three factors: genetics, parenting and trauma. What do they have in common? They are all things that happen to us, not things that we do. If you suffer from social anxiety, the first thing you need to realize is that *it is not your fault*. There's no need to feel guilty. It's the way you are.

But you don't have to stay that way. So let's move on and look at how you can learn to overcome social anxiety and lead a happier, more fulfilled and sociable life.

Chapter 2:
It's All in the Mindset

Before we look at specific treatments and tips for overcoming social anxiety, let's take a minute to look at things from another perspective: inside your mind.

No doubt you've heard people saying, perhaps impatiently, "It's all in your mind! No one's thinking or saying these things about you!" Maybe you've even told yourself that. So why do we continue to believe that other people are criticizing the way we look, how we dress and speak, and the things we say? And why does it matter so much to us what others think?

How low can you go?

The reason why you continue to imagine other people are criticizing you is down to your low self-esteem. You have such a poor image of yourself that you believe all these negative opinions are true. Maybe you feel it's your appearance: your hair, your face, your clothes, or your height is wrong. Maybe it's your behavior, the way you speak to people, or relate to others, or handle a meeting. It might even be something like your social situation that you feel sets you apart. Your thinking (although you may not realize it) is that if other people think negatively about you it's only fair because that's what you deserve – it's all true, in other words.

Why do you think this way? Well, your mind may have been programmed to think like this since you were a child. Your subconscious has been feeding you negative thoughts for years, and now that way of looking at yourself has become a habit.

In other cases this low opinion of yourself may have originated with something that happened to you, such as divorce or bankruptcy. The way you used to see yourself has changed and you now struggle with a lack of confidence and a negative outlook on life. Again you're bombarded with a constant stream of unhelpful thoughts.

Considering low self-esteem is associated with weakness and inferiority, it has some pretty powerful effects. It can lead not only to anxiety and lack of confidence but to anger, mental health issues and self-abuse through food, alcohol and drugs. It gives you a poor self-image and teaches you that you are worthless, so then you end up behaving that way.

We all have a basic need to be accepted; we want people to like us, find us clever or amusing, or respect our talents and position. That's why it matters to us what other people think. It hurts to feel criticized or overlooked, and some of us put immense pressure on ourselves so that we fit in. There's safety in numbers.

Mary had been brought up in care and had no one to guide her after she left school. Her first few jobs were in housekeeping, but after a few years she got a job in an office working with other people. When she started she didn't notice at first that her clothes and appearance were different to theirs. Then she realized the other young women were making fun of her because she looked like she was still a schoolgirl. It was mortifying.

As soon as she could afford to, Mary went out and bought some more suitable clothes, shoes, and lipstick, and got her hair done. After some very difficult months she began to fit in and make friends. Later she could even look back on those hurtful comments and be grateful because they taught her she had to adapt.

Time to change

So some criticism can be helpful, and of course not everyone worries all the time about social occasions and how to fit in. What about people who are okay in most situations, but go to pieces when faced with something too big for them to handle? Even if you have a pretty healthy self-image, you may still feel nervous and jittery when you face a particular task.

The number one issue that most people fear is public speaking, which of course can be a daunting prospect. This could be anything from a relatively minor event, like awarding a school trophy or presenting a report to your colleagues, right up to giving a speech at a big wedding or a society dinner. The thought may be terrifying. No doubt you keep imagining all the things that could go wrong and cringe every time you go through all the scenarios in your head.

Stop! If you keep playing on negative thought patterns, either about yourself or about a situation you face, you're only strengthening those beliefs of low self-worth and your inability to cope. It's time to switch your focus.

The only way to resolve your social anxiety is to change your mindset. All the available treatment options are based on helping to make you feel better about yourself or a specific situation you face, either consciously or subconsciously.

In the next few chapters we'll be having a look at how you can change your way of thinking. It's not easy overcoming something you've believed for so long, and some of us will always have issues around other people, but you can learn to see yourself in a new light and find your place in society.

Chapter 3:
Fight Those Negative Thoughts

At the root of social anxiety is fear. This is not actually fear of other people or a specific situation, but a fear of being studied, observed or humiliated in public. All the different forms of treatment for social anxiety disorder are aimed at teaching you to overcome this fear in various ways.

If you have social anxiety disorder you may be so scared at the thought of being observed, criticized and embarrassed that you avoid situations where this might happen. Chances are you stay away or take other evasive actions that might relieve the pressure in the short term but really only serve to increase the fear.

As we've seen, social anxiety is generally caused by low self-esteem, which is fed by a continuous supply of negative thoughts about ourselves, and the situations we dread. Now it's time to start seeing things differently by learning to identify and challenge our negative way of thinking.

Identify your negative thought patterns

As we saw in the last chapter, the key here is learning a new way of thinking about yourself and the kind of social situations you find so difficult. Identifying your negative thoughts is a great first step to overcoming social anxiety. It helps you see how you are trapped inside a big thought process based on fear and habit that is doing you harm and preventing you developing as a person.

According to the website helpguide.org, negative thought patterns involve a lot of assumptions about a situation and what other people are thinking about you. These can be summarized as mindreading (guessing what's going through their thoughts), fortune telling (predicting what's going to happen), catastrophizing (making things seem a lot worse than they are) and personalizing (assuming that everything is about you).

Let's look at these in more detail.

Mindreading: this is where we assume we know what someone else is thinking. In fact, how many times have you said to yourself in so many words, "I know what she's thinking..." and then added something negative? In fact the other person could be miles away in their thoughts; they just happen to be looking towards you. Or they could even be thinking something favorable about you.

Fortune telling: all too often we confidently predict the future – again in a negative way. Despite our lack of confidence in other areas, our ability to foretell what's going to happen is amazing! "I just know it's going to go wrong." "You can be 100% sure I won't be able to talk to anyone." Does this sound familiar?

Catastrophizing: this is a tendency to get things out of proportion. Say you forgot a key document for a meeting. "It was a disaster! The whole thing was a complete waste of time, and I've blown any chance of promotion for the next five years. I'll be lucky to keep my job!" Actually, it was a nuisance but you were able to cover the main points and then you emailed the document to everyone straight afterwards. Try not to make things worse than they really are.

Personalizing: it's tempting to take everything personally when we have low self-esteem. It could be a comment in a group setting, or your boss warning everyone about some misdemeanor. "She was looking right at me when she said that!" Sometimes it's the opposite. "He wasn't looking at me, but I just know he was getting at me!" At times you may be right, but not always. Don't assume people are criticizing you all the time. Not everything is about you.

Challenge your negative thoughts

Identifying negative thought patterns is a great first step. The next step is to challenge the thoughts you identify. Fighting these thoughts doesn't mean simply denying they exist. You should first recognize these thoughts as negative and harmful, and then attempt to analyze and rebuff them. The best way is to question what they tell you.

Negative thoughts may be along the lines of "I can't do it – I'm going to look like an idiot." Maybe you try to tell yourself "No, it's all going to be fine." Although it may be helpful, this is based on denial. It's better to acknowledge the thought and fight back.

For example, you might catch yourself thinking, "I can't do this presentation at work; I'm going to start stammering and look completely stupid. We'll end up losing the contract and the business will go bust." Acknowledge that this is a negative thought and identify it if you can from the above list: in this case, a mixture of fortune-telling and catastrophizing. You are predicting the future and making your predictions into a catastrophe.

Once you've identified it, you can then ask yourself questions that challenge this view: "How do I know that I'm going to fail? Will other people really think badly of me just because I'm nervous?" Start looking at the problem logically and try to see a more realistic version of the situation in place of the negative thoughts.

Identifying and challenging negative thoughts are two powerful steps towards overcoming social anxiety. These steps are used by counselors and therapists, along with various other treatments, and are key elements in the therapy called Cognitive Behavioral Therapy.

Chapter 4:
Lifestyle Changes for Social Healing

Now you've started on the road to transforming your thought processes, what other steps can you take to beat social anxiety? Well, there are quite a few practical things you can do to help yourself.

What happens when you're faced with one of those social situations you hate? You start experiencing some pretty awful symptoms like feeling dizzy or breathless; you might get tight in the chest, with trembling or weakness in the arms or legs. Maybe you get hot and sweaty or pale and clammy, with nausea, butterflies or an upset stomach. It can be impossible to conceal your symptoms; in fact, one of the worst elements is imagining those around you noticing what's going on. For some reason this thought makes everything ten times worse.

In this chapter we're going to look at how you can make a big difference to your social anxiety by making a few changes to your way of life.

Breathing exercises

Learn some breathing exercises and practice them at home. Once you've learned to control your breathing you can use this skill very successfully to ward off those feelings of panic, trembling, shortness of breath, racing pulse and dizziness when you're in a social setting.

It's important to slow down your breathing in stressful situations because it will help you stay calm. Breathing too fast can lead to an imbalance of oxygen and carbon dioxide, making you feel more anxious.

You can try out various breathing exercises until you find what works best for you. It should be something fairly subtle so that you can use the technique with other people around. One of the simplest involves breathing in for a count of five, and then breathing out for a count of seven. Practice on your own and then use it whenever you face a situation where you're not comfortable.

Relax!

Another useful idea is to learn a relaxation technique. Sign up for a local class and you may well meet other people with anxiety issues. Books, videos and DVDs can all help, but a qualified professional is best if you want to learn something like yoga. You could try jogging, swimming, walking or take up a relaxing hobby to help you de-stress.

Some relaxation techniques are as simple as visualizing something peaceful and calming; it could be your dream vacation island, a fantasy landscape, a favorite view or even just a cozy item of clothing. These simple ideas have the benefit of being totally transferrable to any stressful social situation. You can combine them with your breathing exercise and put them into practice before and even during a social activity to ward off some of the distressing symptoms like dizziness, tightness in the chest, and rapid pulse.

You should also cut down or eliminate stimulants, including caffeine, nicotine and alcohol, which actually make you jittery. Maybe you thought that cigarettes and alcohol help you relax before a social event, but they are both stimulating substances and are likely to make your anxiety worse.

Make sure you get enough sleep. Try to relax in the evenings before you go to bed and clear your mind of any anxious thoughts. It may help to keep a diary so that before you go to bed you can note down anything that's likely to keep you awake by replaying in your mind. Once it's on paper you can forget it. Have a warm bath or a milky drink to help you sleep.

Form new relationships

It may seem a strange idea since social relationships are part of the problem, but you should try to get to know more people. If you suffer from social anxiety, chances are you have a very limited circle of friends and acquaintances. Maybe you're pretty isolated. The best thing you can do is to join a small supportive group and get to know people. It's a great way to become more confident.

You could consider taking an assertiveness course, for example, or volunteering with a charity. Many organizations are desperate for volunteers, and you could learn new skills as well as helping out a worthwhile cause. If you don't want to face the public you could work behind the scenes in some way, or with animals at a rescue center if you don't want to spend all the time with people.

Anne was an elementary school teacher who had suffered a breakdown and lost all confidence in herself. As well as seeing a therapist she was helped by members of a local church, which happened to be right next door to the home she shared with her mother. Anne struggled for several years before agreeing to help out at a children's group at the church, initially just by playing the piano. She began to build up her confidence and was eventually able to return to teaching.

Go walking

You might like to consider getting a dog if you have the time to care for one. Walking a dog every day can make a big difference to your mental and physical health, your ability to relax and your confidence in talking to strangers, because dog walkers who see each other every day often stop and talk. Other people will also speak to you and admire your dog even if they don't own one. Who knows? There could be a whole community of friendly dog lovers out there for you to join.

Get professional help

Do you feel you need more support? You should see a doctor or therapist if you suffer from a more serious form of social anxiety. Counseling is very effective in treating social anxiety disorder, so there's no need to feel embarrassed or say, "It's not for me." Treatment is likely to be based on the type of solutions we've been looking at, along with anything else specific to your needs. It may also involve some group sessions, role play, and so on.

Your doctor may prescribe medication to help you while you recover. These drugs should only be used as a last resort and together with other forms of treatment. Medication does not actually cure social anxiety but acts as a temporary solution to help you manage your condition; it could aid in overcoming panic attacks, for example. It can be very useful in the short term, but it's vital to get your anxiety issues resolved to be sure of a permanent cure.

Chapter 5:

Face up to Your Fears

It may be tempting to hide away and avoid anything that makes you feel bad, but it's not going to help in the long run. Facing up to the things that make you nervous is the best way of learning to overcome them. In this chapter we're going to be looking at ways to tackle the things we fear one by one.

The social anxiety ladder

Make a list of all the social events or tasks you find most difficult. Then put them in order, starting with the most difficult and going down to the relatively simple. Some experts call this "the social anxiety ladder." (It's sometimes suggested you put the easiest things at the top of the list but with this one, like all good ladders, you climb up from the bottom.)

Your ladder may look something like this:

- *Addressing a roomful of people*

- *A social evening at the Country Club*

- *Joining co-workers for a drink*

- *Meeting a friend for coffee in town*

- *Going to the supermarket*

Maybe your ladder is long and it looks like a very daunting climb. Don't worry – just focus on the "easiest" of the events you've listed. We'll assume it's something like going shopping for groceries (to the mall, not online!).

You probably have your own way of coping with this sort of task. Many people with social anxiety have rigid rules they impose on themselves in an attempt to control the situation. At times it's an effort just to get as far as the bottom rung! But when it comes to actually climbing the ladder, we often have to bend those rules and move out of our comfort zone on every rung, one tiny bit at a time.

How can you take a tiny step out of your comfort zone in your local supermarket? Well, many people don't talk to the checkout staff, but as a first little step you could make an effort to greet them and make one simple, non-essential remark. The easiest thing is to say something like, "Lovely day, isn't it?" The comment could be about the product you're buying or the amount of people in the store. Making your comment into a question is a great way of getting a response.

Whatever your lowest rung on the ladder, and however you choose to tackle it, keep practicing your task until it comes naturally. Then make another little change; maybe ask where a product is in the store, or speak to another customer. Keep working away, one tiny bit at a time, until you're feeling comfortable about your bottom rung and ready to step up.

Each task should be broken down into steps in this way so that you gain confidence before moving on. For example, if you don't like the thought of socializing in large groups you could try going with a more confident friend and just make a point of speaking to one other person. Once you're comfortable with that, move on to talking to two people, and so on.

These changes will take time; don't try to do everything at once. You run the risk of becoming despondent and making the situation worse! Just take little steps, beginning with the issues you find the least scary and gradually working your way up the ladder once you've become more confident.

Boost your self-confidence

Every little change will be a great confidence booster. Try keeping a record of what you accomplish, so you can look back and see how far you've come. Think up a reward system too, preferably not based on alcohol or too many calories!

Matilda had a lot of anxiety issues and poor self-confidence. It took her a long time to start working her way up the ladder. She built a great reward system around her love of clothes, buying stylish skirts, jackets or shoes she could wear to work every time she reached a new goal. She would also award herself smaller treats, like getting casual accessories or new makeup, for the minor changes she made. Not only was this method a practical way of rewarding herself, but her new image gave her confidence a big boost every time she saw herself in a mirror.

Make the most of your potential. How you feel about yourself is important, so avoid using negative language to describe yourself. Don't say, "I always get things wrong," and so on. Some people with social anxiety end up letting themselves go and say it doesn't matter what they look like. It does matter! Make the most of your appearance by keeping yourself clean and neat, and stick to your ideal weight. Try to walk tall and be proud of yourself.

Consider taking a course. A social skills course teaches you about appropriate behaviors in social settings and how to put them into practice. You can learn how to introduce yourself and make small talk, for example. An assertiveness course could also help you learn to be more confident by showing you how to stand up for yourself politely and get others to take you seriously.

Make up a mantra. Many people find it helps to have a mantra to repeat to help them see themselves in a constructive way. Analyze your positive qualities (get a friend to help you if necessary) and sum up the way you aim to see yourself in the not too distant future. You could write a few words, or a whole passage, about the attributes and abilities you want to emphasize and repeat them every day. For example, you might say, "I'm a calm, rational person who is great at her job, kind to other people and a stunning redhead!"

Own yourself. You don't have to go through life trying to be someone else. Be proud of who you are and what you can do. Some people are good with kids, or baking cakes, or making money or designing computer games. You may not be the world's best conversationalist, but you're great at something.

James was a shy child and grew up into a reserved adult who found it difficult to talk to people and preferred the world of books. When he lost his job in the recession he struggled to get work. In desperation he decided to become self-employed and started using his talents to write articles and books for clients around the world via the Internet. Although his earnings were modest, he found he had become confident because he'd learned to use his strengths.

Focus on your good points, accept your faults, count your blessings and learn to like yourself. As Judy Garland once said, "Always be the first rate version of yourself, instead of a second rate version of someone else."

Watch out for others. Your experience and struggles should mean you are able to empathize with other people who have confidence issues. They are more likely to turn to someone like you who understands what they're going through than someone who's bold and outgoing. You may not win on the popularity stakes, but you can be a good, kind friend to plenty of other people and might even find you're their role model.

Chapter 6:
How to Walk into a Room

A key problem for anyone with social anxiety is the fear that everyone's looking at them. This is strongest when they have to enter a room full of people – especially when everyone else is sitting down – but it can apply to any situation.

Self-consciousness is at the root of social anxiety, because it's closely linked to the dread of being observed, assessed, criticized and humiliated. But are people really staring? Is there anything we can do to stop them? And how can we learn to brave their stares?

According to the website peopleskillsdecoded.com, sometimes it's true; people are staring at you! There are two reasons why this happens. Firstly, it could be that there's something odd about your appearance, in which case you can quite easily work out whether anything can be done about it. Remember Mary in Chapter 2 with her inappropriate work clothes?

The second reason may be that because of your social anxiety you are going about with a frightened expression on your face. If you look pale with wide open eyes and nervous mannerisms, for example, it will attract attention.

The website goes on to point out that quite often the idea that everyone is staring at you all the time is actually untrue. It's just part of the social anxiety we're trying to overcome. So whether real or imagined, how do we cope with those stares when we walk down the street or into a room?

Win yourself an Oscar

If you enter a room thinking about yourself you become awkward and clumsy. You may hunch your shoulders and drop your head. You might hide behind someone or something. You'll probably fiddle with your clothes because you feel inadequately dressed. Your body language signals you're embarrassed and uncomfortable, which in itself can draw attention to you.

Now imagine a famous Hollywood star walking up to the stage to collect an Oscar. Do you imagine for one moment they're not nervous of letting themselves down – especially on live TV in front of millions of viewers? They're just good at acting. So try it for yourself and start acting calm and in control. The difference can be amazing.

Angela and Daphne were both attending a big family wedding. The time came to pose for some group photos, but Daphne was battling with feelings of inadequacy and tried to get out of it. Angela went to reassure her. "I know how you feel," she confided, "because I'm just the same. But it only makes you more conspicuous if you let it show. You just have to brazen it out."

Daphne couldn't believe Angela was nervous too; she'd known her for years without suspecting it was all an act.

Stop focusing on yourself

You don't want other people to focus their attention on you, so don't do it to yourself either! Remember, up to the second before you enter a room everyone was just going about their daily life; checking their emails, looking out the window, talking to friends, wondering what their kids are up to or what to have for dinner. When you walked in some may have glanced up but their attention isn't really on you.

Peter had a dread of being looked at by others. He didn't know how to handle it. One day he was given a vital piece of advice by his brother as they got on a bus together, which he remembered for the rest of his life. "They're not interested in you. They're *like* you – only interested in themselves!"

Slow down

Don't walk in and then rush to find a seat or quiet corner unless you're running late for a meeting. Someone in a hurry always attracts attention. It might go against your instincts, but make yourself walk casually. You're more likely to be able to speak calmly too if you've managed to make yourself appear composed.

Find a distraction

When you wish the floor would open up and swallow you, or you're desperately wishing you were anywhere else, distract yourself by looking at your surroundings. Analyze the décor or concentrate on anything that catches your attention, like a bug crawling up a wall or a stain on the carpet. Ask someone a question to switch the focus away from you; become a good listener and really pay attention to other people.

Smile, smile, smile

Remember that Hollywood star claiming an Oscar? They might not manage much of a speech, but their smile says it all. Same with us; we can use a smile to make us look relaxed and calm (even when we're not) and as a way of acknowledging people without having to start a conversation.

Scientists believe that when we smile we start to feel better. That's because smiling releases endorphins in the brain that lift our mood. What's more, it's a great way to relax those muscles that tense up when we're nervous.

Learn to laugh at yourself

Take the smiling one step further and learn to laugh at your awkwardness. It's not the same as putting yourself down;

think of it more as putting other people at ease.

Maybe your shoes squeak as you cross a silent room, you drop a whole pile of books or the whole area suddenly goes quiet just as you speak. This could happen to anyone, so there's no need to be embarrassed. You could just say something like "Perfect timing! Don't you hate it when that happens?" "Oops! There I go again!" or "Don't mind me! Just making myself at home..." This is self-deprecation, and by laughing you invite others to laugh with you, not at you.

A little boy cycled into the local park and fell off his bike in front of a couple of strangers. With perfect composure he picked himself off, got back on his bike and remarked casually, "I always do that when I come here!"

Job interviews

Going for a job interview is daunting for just about everyone, so don't feel you're on your own here. Prepare in advance by finding out everything you can about the company and the position you're interviewing for. Dress smartly and make the most of your appearance – if you look good you'll have more confidence. Try to walk in with your head high and shake hands firmly.

The worst question for anyone with social anxiety is the dreaded "Tell us about yourself" type. Again the best thing is to prepare in advance. Remember, they don't really want to learn everything about you; just sum up your situation in a few sentences. What they really want to know is how well you could do the job, so tie in any experiences you've had with the demands of the role. Make notes or even write it all out in full, explaining before you read it that you wanted to make sure you missed nothing out. If your hands are shaky, lay the notes on the table or on your lap instead of holding them.

If the interviewers mention that others have described you as reserved and quiet, turn this into a positive. For example, you could explain your strengths lie in observing, analyzing and planning, or use the opportunity to highlight your focus and attention to detail, and give an instance (which you've also prepared in advance) of how this has benefited you professionally. If they know that your social anxiety has been a problem in the past, be honest and explain how you're working on it.

Chapter 7:
The Secret Art of Small Talk

One of the most difficult things for anyone who is shy, nervous or suffering from social anxiety phobia is talking to people. Yet dialogue is at the center of almost all human interactions, so it's vital to be able to communicate.

Every day millions of us have casual meetings with strangers or slight acquaintances where we simply exchange polite remarks for a few minutes. This is known as small talk, and to anyone with social anxiety it can be a whole new language to learn. How can we overcome our fear of having to make conversation?

Identify the problem

Although this can be a general awkwardness involving any conversation in any setting, it's more usually in relation to specific events or people. We may say we can't talk to *anyone*, but after a little thought we can often amend such a sweeping statement. We don't usually get nervous or tongue-tied chatting to our close family members or a good friend, for example. So that implies the problem lies in talking to people we don't know very well, or at all.

You may be able to narrow it down further. Maybe you can talk to kids, but not to their parents. Maybe you find it easier to get on with people you consider socially below you. This suggests you can talk to these groups because you don't feel challenged by them. Or perhaps you can make small talk to a stranger provided there's only one person at a time, or it's in a certain type of environment; this would mean it's the number of people or the setting that puts you off. If you can analyze the problem in this way, you may feel pleasantly surprised that actually it's not as bad as you feared.

Don't stress about silence

One of the things we fear about trying to have a conversation with someone is the thought of long pauses while we struggle desperately to think of something to say. This is a common problem.

The secret is to have a few topics or phrases that you've thought of in advance. Talk about the weather or the surroundings, or ask about their family or plans for vacations, but try not to fire off a whole load of questions or it will turn into an interview! It's good to listen and take an interest in what the other person says. You should respond to the answers and say a little bit about yourself when appropriate. Don't feel you have to fill all the silences; it's a conversation, so the other person also has to do their part.

Play the game

Imagine two closely matched people playing tennis. If either one of them fails to return the ball over the net they're in danger of losing the game, so the shots will probably come thick and fast. That's how conversation is between two confident, outgoing people who may have known each other for years.

Now imagine you're one of the players but your opponent is a child of about six. The rules have changed subtly; instead of getting the ball back at all costs you want to return it gently, within reach. There's less effort but still you have to pay close attention. This is small talk between strangers. You want to keep it going to be polite, but it's never going to last long.

You could start by "serving" one of your standard phrases, which you've learned in advance. It's usually safe to talk about the weather, for example. You may say, "I hope the weather improves in time for the vacation. It's so disappointing when it's like this isn't it?" (Remember what we said about making comments into questions?) After the other person responds you should follow up on their answer, perhaps by mentioning your plans for the holidays and adding something like "Have you been there?"

Remember to respond to their efforts without just saying Yes or No, because one-word answers kill a conversation. We want to get the ball back over the net. The easiest way is to turn the question back on them. For example, they may ask you if you've ever been to a certain holiday destination. Instead of just saying No, you could say "No, but it sounds fantastic" or "No, but I'd love to some day" and ask them to tell you more about it.

Pay a compliment

Paying a compliment is a great way to start a conversation, even with someone you've only just met. You can say, for example, "I love your necklace! Where did you get it?" This could be the opener to a whole discussion on jewelry, accessories and gifts. The only times when it doesn't work is straight after a long pause when you've been trying to think of something to say (a compliment has to be as genuine and spontaneous as possible) and when the item you choose to admire is not really admirable at all on closer inspection!

If someone pays you a compliment, the correct response is to thank them. Don't put them down by dismissing their praise or saying you've had the item for years. Get that ball back over the net as graciously as possible.

Become more interesting

If you're the sort of person who doesn't go out much and has a limited social life, other people might find it difficult to know what to talk about with you. Make sure you're well informed about current affairs or local interest stories. Take up a hobby or do a class in a subject that interests you; not only will you meet more people with similar interests, but your wider range of activities will always give you something to share with others.

Practice makes perfect

There's nothing like regular use to help you improve your communication skills, so do keep trying. It may be difficult but it's worth the effort. Combine this with the hints on breathing and relaxation exercises and developing self-confidence, and there's no reason why you shouldn't end up speaking fluent small talk!

Conclusion

Thank you for reading my book. I hope you now have a greater understanding of Social Anxiety and the steps you can take to remove the anxiety from your life.

Hopefully you have found the root cause of your social fears and you can now begin to take action and start living the life that you really desire. I know how debilitating social anxiety and shyness can be to your life, because I too once struggled with it. I overcame these fears and so can you!

I promise you that if you really take the suggestions in this book to heart and apply them to your life things will begin to get better for you. Of course simply reading something and not taking action will never get you where you want to be—no matter what the subject. You must take real action to succeed at anything!

I wish you all the best and many years of prosperity and happiness.

I'm always surprised at the amount of people that confuse shyness with simply being an introvert. If you think you may be an introvert be sure to check out my book 'The Introvert Mindset: How to Use Your Special Talents and Unique Personality Traits to Create Success.'

Printed in Great Britain
by Amazon